12 SIMPLE TECHNICAL INDICATORS
THAT REALLY WORK

Mark Larson

Marketplace Books
Columbia, Maryland

This book, along with other books, is available at discounts that make it realistic to provide them as gifts to your customers, clients, and staff. For more information on these long lasting, cost effective premiums, please call us at 800-272-2855 or e-mail us at sales@traderslibrary.com.

ISBN: 1-59280-290-7
ISBN 13: 978-1-59280-290-6
Printed in the United States of America.

Table of Contents

12 Simple Technical Indicators that Really Work

FROM THE PUBLISHER

The editors at Marketplace Books have always kept a steady goal in mind, and that is to present actionable information on stock trading in the most straight-forward, practical medium available. Sometimes this involves a book, sometimes a newsletter, a DVD, or an online course program. What we've learned from the many products we've developed over the years is that a cross-medium approach is the most effective way to offer the greatest possible value to our readers.

So an idea was born. This innovative book and DVD set is one of the first in a series that combines a full course book derived from the actual presentation itself. Our idea grew out of a simple question. Students of stock trading spend a great deal of their own money attending lectures and trade shows. After all the travel, effort, and expense, that student will still have to assimilate a host of often complex theories and strategies. Sometimes he or she may want to ask a question or dig deeper into an issue, but they hold back; maybe because they still don't know enough about the bigger picture or maybe they don't even know some of the basic terminology. They may buy the DVD, but still...a lecture in itself is not a comprehensive learning tool and a person may still need yet another lecture or host of trial and error book purchases to master the subject.

So the question was: Does the average student of trading get enough out of an individual session to effectively carry their studies home and master a subject? The answer was a resounding no! Most attendees get bits and pieces of the message out of a long and expensive lineage of lectures, with critical details hopefully captured in page after page of scribbled notes. For those who are gifted with a photographic memory and vast organizational skills, the visual lecture is just fine, but for the rest of us, the combination of the written word and a visual demonstration is the golden ticket to the mastery of any subject.

A comprehensive approach to learning is the course you are about to embark upon. We've taken Mark Larson's original lecture and extracted his core content into an easy to read and understand course book. You'll be able to pour over every word of Larson's groundbreaking presentation, taking in each important point in a step by step, layer by layer process. All of this is possible because our editors have developed this title in classic textbook form. We've organized and highlighted the key points, added case studies, glossaries, key terms, and even an index so you can go to the information you need when you need it most.

Let's face it, stock trading in any medium takes years to master. It takes time to be able to follow charts and pick out the indicators that mark the wins you'll need to succeed. And beyond the mathematical details and back-tested chart patterns, every presenter has three very basic premises for every student trader; they are to control your emotions, stay close to your trading plan, and do your homework. It's so important to know the full picture of the profession because it could either make you rich or put you in line for that second night job.

This DVD course book package is meant to give you all the visual and written reinforcement you need to study, memorize, document, and master your subject once and for all. We think this is a truly unique approach to realizing the full potential of our Traders' Library DVDs.

As always, we wish you the greatest success.

Meet Mark Larson

Mark Larson is a seasoned trader, weekly writer for www.incometrader.com, and educator who has been actively trading the markets since 1998. His courses on technical analysis and the use of technical indicators are sought after by many traders. His simple trading skills have helped thousands of investors of all types make money during an up, down, or sideways market.

His best selling DVD courses include *12 Simple Indicators That Really Work*, and his best selling books include *Technical Charting for Profits* and *Trade Stocks Online*. With the use of technical indicators, Mark was able to warn investors of the last bear market correction that occurred in 2000, and again warns investors to be careful of the next up and coming correction. One of Mark's coined phrases has always been that the "key to success is knowing when to buy and when to sell," which can only be done with the use of technical indicators.

Mark is the founder of Rolling Along Investments and an instructor for Investools. He travels throughout the country teaching others how to become independent investors by using both technical indicators and options. He attributes most of his skills and success to his very successful mentors Mike D. Coval and Stacy G. Acevedo.

Introduction

Consider the following short statement from author Mark Larson:

> "Then came April 2000, when the bull decided to quit running and appeared to give in to the bear as we began a true stock market correction, one that many investors never experienced before.
>
> This wasn't just a short-term monthly correction; it truly was a bearish correction that would stay with us for many months. This bearish correction created big problems for thousands and thousands of investors who didn't have the right mindset and knowledge of what to do or how to react."

Larson had just finished writing the book *Technical Charting for Profits* that contained this statement in April 2000. It was released in January 2001. The market then continued lower by about 50%

before stopping in March 2003 and moving higher as the Dow Jones broke through the previous high of about 12,500 and reached 13,600 by mid June of 2007. Now the question is will it go higher or lower? Only technical indicators will tell us that! Read on and find out which technical indicators are Mark's favorites now.

The Goal of This Book

The purpose of Larson's text is to help you understand the power of technical indicators and the right parameters. There are over 200 different types of technical indicators out there, and he shows you a list of the ones that are most commonly used. As you read, Larson asks that you keep this important point in mind.

Basically, a parameter is a number. Think of the number in terms of your mother's prized cake recipe. When she bakes that cake, what would happen if she leaves out one of the key ingredients, like the flour? Or if the recipe calls for half a cup of flour and she adds only a quarter-cup? It would make a big difference.

What Larson describes to you here are the technical indicators that he's found work well and consistently—regardless of whether

The key to investing in the stock market when using technical indicators is finding the right parameters.

the market is bullish or bearish—as long as you slightly modify the parameters. Figure 1.1 on page 3 shows an example of the indicators that you'll learn about throughout this book.

Although Larson admits to being far from the best investor in the stock market, he's been very successful at making money for a living for the past several years. And he attributes this success to a single factor: his focus on technical indicators and the right parameters. As a two time best selling author and writer of a weekly commentary www.incometrader.com, he has a simple process for helping others become successful. Read on to discover how he can help you too.

12 SIMPLE TECHNICAL INDICATORS

THAT REALLY WORK

Chapter 1

Technical Indicators 101

One thing I've always believed is that technical indicators are more important than fundamentals. Time and again, I've seen that the proper use of technical indicators enables investors to determine which stocks to buy or sell and—more importantly—when to do it.

Power of Parameters

To effectively utilize technical indicators, you must first understand that the most essential aspects of these indicators are their parameters. This is because proper parameters offer you better entry and exit points.

> *Technical indicators are more important than fundamentals.*

Two Main Types of Technical Indicators

The list in Figure 1.1 demonstrates some of the different types of technical indicators. But by no means should you think that this list is entirely comprehensive. Rather, dozens more indicators exist, including support levels, moving averages, linear regression lines, volume bars, stochastics, ease of movement, average true range, and so on. There are three leading indicators I want to bring to your attention in Figure 1.1: time-segmented volume (TSV©), money stream, and balance of power (BOP©). I also want to bring two different styles of indicators to your attention:

- Lagging indicators, which basically move after prices move

- Leading indicators, which change before prices change

You're probably pretty familiar with the three indicators I've starred in figure 1.1 because they're included in Worden Brothers' TC 2000©. I've been using the TC 2000© for many years because I believe it to be one of the premier charting services available. I find the TC 2000© to be extremely powerful because it focuses on these three leading indicators, which are based on price movement and volume. Also I have found that other indicators such as ease of movement and average true range (prophet.net) indicators are extremely helpful too.

FIGURE 1.1

Technical Indicators

Support Levels	**Resistance Levels**
Moving Averages	**Bolling_r Bands**
Linear Regression Lines	**MACD**
Volume Bars	**Balance of Power ***
Stochastics	**Price Rate of Change**
Time Segmented Volume *	**Relative Strength**
Money Stream *	**Wilders RSI**

* Leading Indicators

The Leading Role That Volume Plays

Let's talk about volume for a moment. It's really important to remember that volume goes with the trend. This means that it's normal for volume to increase as prices increase and to decrease as prices decrease—which you see occurring in Figure 1.2.

> *Volume plays an absolutely essential role in the stock market.*

When volume is moving with the trend in the direction of the price, it's telling you one thing and one thing only. This crucial piece of information is that the prevailing trend is healthy and that it's a good relationship.

When prices are declining, and you see a corresponding decline in volume, don't panic! Keep in mind that it's normal for volume to decline as well.

This means that downside breakouts from price patterns often occur with relatively low volume. If volume expands as prices decline, this emphasizes the bearishness of the breakout. That's because circum-stances in which declining prices couple with expanding volume rep-resent overall greater enthusiasm

> *Increased volume is often greater than the average volume over the past 20 trading days.*

among sellers. More volume basically means more sellers during a downtrend and more volume in an uptrend means more buyers; and as we all know, more is better because it will force the price of the stock to move further.

Evolution of Mark Larson's Trading Style

I've been trading in the market since I was 24 years old. The only dif-ference between then and now—and I'm 42—is that I now use techni-cal indicators, which I've done for the last 10 years. When I was in real estate at age 24, I was taught that you should always buy and hold. Unfortunately, I started seeing some of my assets head in the wrong direction. So I began to take a more aggressive approach, managing my own money. I learned that there are times when you should sell some of your best stocks, which you may have had for a long time, and there are other times when you should buy some that you've never, ever considered buying before. The only way I could identify those stocks was by using technical indicators, as well as scans/searches. We'll discuss scans/searches a bit later in chapter 10, when I give you an easy way to follow and track them.

As with all upside breakouts, volume is key. It must expand be-yond the breakout to indicate enthusiasm. Therefore, a change in the supply and demand is in favor of demand. So it follows that volume has a major impact on what individual stocks or the index itself will do.

Figure 1.2 provides an example of an uptrend. You see that I've drawn a lot of vertical lines. Believe it or not, some stocks still go up—and others still go down. That said, I can tell you that the most successful traders really don't care if the stock market goes up, down, or sideways. You may have heard the saying, "The stock market drops

FIGURE 1.2

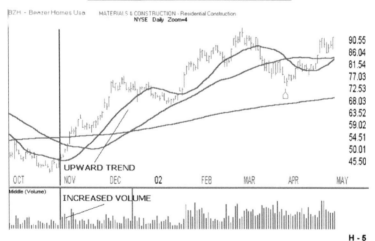

UPWARD TREND

BZH - Beazer Homes Usa   MATERIALS & CONSTRUCTION - Residential Construction
NYSE Daily Zoom=4

90.55
86.04
81.54
77.03
72.53
68.03
63.52
59.02
54.51
50.01
45.50

UPWARD TREND

OCT   NOV   DEC   02   FEB   MAR   APR   MAY

Middle (Volume)

INCREASED VOLUME

H - 5

For color charts go to www. traderslibrary.com/TLEcorner

four to eight times faster than it goes up." We've certainly witnessed that in the past, most recently at the latter part of 1989 and of 1999. But as Figure 1.2 shows, we had an upward trend with a corresponding increase in volume.

In Figure 1.3, you see the breakout again, with yet another upward movement.

It shows that the trend was moving in an upward direction, with a positive increase in volume. So as the saying goes, make the trend your friend!

FIGURE 1.3

VOLUME BREAK OUT

For color charts go to www. traderslibrary.com/TLEcorner

Chapter Summary

• Technical indicators are more important than fundamentals.

• Technical indicators and their corresponding parameters tell you what to buy, what to sell, and more importantly when.

• Proper parameters help you to determine when to enter the market—and when to exit.

• The two types of technical indicators are lagging and leading.

• Volume plays an essential role in technical indicators, increasing and decreasing along with price trends.

• In an environment with declining prices, it's normal to see a subsequent decline in volume.

• When volume increases and prices decline, that is an indication that sellers are more enthusiastic.

Self-test questions

1. Why are technical indicators better than fundamentals?

   a. Technical indicators are statistically driven and always right
   b. They allow you to find potential stocks, and more importantly, tell you when to buy and sell them
   c. Fundamentals are always lagging
   d. Fundamentals work best in long-term buy and hold situations

2. Which of the following is a leading indicator?

   a. Moving averages
   b. Relative strength
   c. Money stream
   d. Stochastics

3. Which of the following statements about volume is false?

   a. It is normal for volume to increase as prices go up
   b. In an upside breakout, if volume expands, that is very favorable for the stock
   c. It is normal for volume to increase as prices decline
   d. If volume increases on a downside breakout, that emphasizes the overall bearishness of the move

4. For more aggressive trading, the author believes that:

   a. Fundamentals trump technicals
   b. You should always buy and hold. Long-term transactions always end up making money
   c. Volume is more important than technical indicators
   d. You should use technical indicators

5. What is the most essential aspect of using technical indicators?

   a.   Proper parameters
   b.   That you never ignore or override their signals
   c.   Volume
   d.   That you use 12 of them

For answers, go to www.traderslibrary.com/TLEcorner

Chapter 2

Moving Averages

A moving average is the sum of whatever you're examining. In this case, I'm talking about the closing prices of a stock. For example, a 20–, 30–, 50–, 100–, or 200-day moving average is then divided by the total number of days, resulting in the average price of the stock. A 30-day period is commonly used for short-term buy and sell signals.

As stocks move above the 30-day moving average, it's said that the stock has greater upside potential; and, as the price drops down below the 30-day moving average it's said that the stock has greater odds of moving lower at that time. Such moving averages are helpful when determining levels of support and resistance. As a habit, I have found that once a stock drops below the 30-day moving average, it may be best to place a stop loss order at a select price. I'll talk more about this in Chapter 9 as I go into the details using the Average True Range (ATR) indicator.

Also keep in mind that of all the various moving averages, the 200-day moving average results in the strongest moving average. This is simply because it is referred to as being a major point of support or resistance for either stocks or Indexes.

Moving Averages Examined

Below is a good example of how to compute a moving average. By adding the closing prices of this stock over the last 7 days, you get $393.93. Divide that result by the 7 days because each one of those numbers represents 1 day. That process results in the average price of the stock—$56.27.

> *Example: $56.06 + $59.31 + $56 + $55.56*
> *+ $56 + $57 and $56.26 = $393.93 Now divide*
> *$393.93 by 7 (total number of days)*
> *= $56.27 average price.*

The first thing to remember about a moving average is not its precise total—but what that total represents. Whichever moving average you're looking at, its total represents the price of that stock over that time frame. So if I'm looking at a 7-day moving average, and I've got $56.27, that tells me that the average price of the stock over the last 7 days was $56.27—because that's the parameter I was using.

Stay focused on the fact that a moving average represents the price of a stock within a certain period. So when using such moving averages as the 30 or even the 200, it's telling you what the average price is for that given time frame.

Looking Back on Moving Averages circa the 1990s

Moving averages have become extremely popular again. I remember in 1997, '98, and '99, the only moving averages people were looking at were 10s and 20s, maybe 30s. The 200-day moving average was so far away from the actual current price of the stock, no one could locate it. As I mention in my book *Technical Charting for Profits*, everyone now looks at 200-day moving averages as the strongest point of support or resistance because stocks continue to change directions. So a 200-day moving average is taking a major toll in the actual evaluation of a stock.

Two Main Types of Moving Averages

There are two primary types of moving averages:

- Simple moving averages include less of a reaction, allowing for a slower or more effective signal.

- Exponential moving averages create more of a reaction, causing a faster and less effective signal.

Various time frames are used in varying market conditions. The shorter the moving average, the faster the movement will be. And the larger the moving average, the slower the movement will be.

Now you're saying to yourself—why should a shorter moving average and faster movement be important to me? A good question: if you're in a bullish position or long in the stock (or maybe just the option), you should probably consider shortening your moving average. Don't keep the moving average the same. If you're using a 30- or 40-day moving average, it's going to take 30 or 40 days before you actually begin getting a sell signal. So by all means, shorten some of those averages!

If you find yourself in a bullish position with the market beginning to change course, consider shortening your moving average—which will result in a quicker sell-signal.

Which Moving Average Does Larson Rely On?

Now that we've covered the differences between simple and exponential moving averages, I will tell you that I almost always use a simple moving average, except with two different indicators. My reason for this is simple: I've found that the exponential moving average with those two indicators works best. And I've back-tested every approach I refer to in this book for a minimum of 6 months before applying it to real money.

FIGURE 2.1

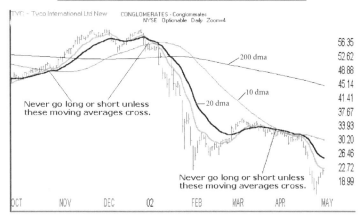

BUY and SELL POINTS

TYC - Tyco International Ltd New   CONGLOMERATES - Conglomerates
                                     NYSE Optionable Daily Zoom=4

200 dma

10 dma

20 dma

Never go long or short unless
these moving averages cross.

Never go long or short unless
these moving averages cross.

56.35
52.62
48.88
45.14
41.41
37.67
33.93
30.20
26.46
22.72
18.99

OCT   NOV   DEC   02   FEB   MAR   APR   MAY

H - 9

For color charts go to www. traderslibrary.com/TLEcorner

These days, people are using shorter moving averages ranging from 10 to 30 days. Why? Because shorter moving averages help investors identify both when to get into or out of a stock sooner rather than later.

A chart on moving averages is shown in Figure 2.1. Though there are four averages here, I'm going to focus on the two larger ones, the 10- and 20- day. Never go long or short unless these moving averages cross. If you go directly up in the chart, you have a cross on these moving averages. When you see the 10-day break down through the 20-day, it would be a short opportunity or a sign of weakness in the stock. If it were the reverse, it would be a buy opportunity or a sign of strength as the 10-day moving average moved up through the 20-day moving average.

Moving Average Time Target: 3 Days

Another factor that you should consider with this moving average is consecutive days. In this example, you should see a specific average confirmed over at least 3 consecutive days, primarily because there was a crossover of the moving averages.

The more pluses your chart shows, the more positive the outlook.

What you see in Figure 2.1 is a simple 10- and 20-day moving average. This is resulting in a short (downward investment) opportunity, right? Not necessarily. I use a 12-plus system, and this is how I've set it up. There are 12 tabs on my charting system. I start by putting the least effective one in tab 1 and the most effective one in tab 12. By the time I go through 1 to 12, if I have more pluses than minuses, I consider taking on the position. You can use various types of technical programs to create your own 12 plus scenario. You may even utilize your most rewarding technical indicators by adding them all on one chart so you can view them at the same time. I do this from time to time by simply saving the setting and giving it a title "MY SYSTEM"—this gives me the ability to quickly review my most prized technical indicators with just the push of a button. If you're interested in all of my prized technical indicators in "MY SYSTEM" and their details, look for my home study course *The Complete Guide to Technical Indicators.*

In this book I will look at moving averages, moving average convergence/divergence (MACD, which I cover in chapter 4), price rate of change (PRC, chapter 5), time-segmented volume (TSV©, chapter 6), and RSI© TSV© (chapter 7). If I can get more plusses—for example, if I look at a chart and see seven plusses—that's a positive. I can then start to consider what type of investment strategy to use with that chart.

If Figure 2.1 were tab 1, I would say that so far, this would be a plus (assuming I wanted to short it). The 10-day has crossed through the 20-day, which is a better signal in this case, and the stock should move lower. But as I said, I would also wait 3 days to see how the trade actually falls out before making a final determination.

Another important consideration in this case is the 200-day moving average. As I discussed at the beginning of this chapter, the 200-day moving average is still the strongest point of support. Although this stock's moving averages are crossed, the fact remains that it's coming down, testing its strongest point of support—so I would still be patient. Wait for it. Get another confirmation.

Once it finally breaks down, I'd have better odds of increasing my return, or at the least, losing less money. Yet another interesting occurrence in a picture like this is when you have a gap up or down (see Figure 2.2). A gap up or down is a sign of strength or weakness. When stocks gap up, the price moved higher

> *Be sure to avoid trading a stock before it comes down far enough to test its strongest point of support, which would be what we refer to as a better confirmation of taking on the trade.*

FIGURE 2.2

Volume with Moving Average

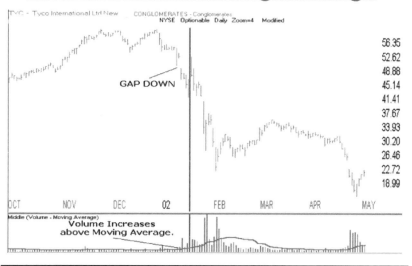

prior to the open of the market; and, when stocks gap down, the price moved lower prior to the market open. This is simply a sign of good (gap up) or bad (gap down) news taking place and the stock market adjusting the price before the open. Stocks that gap up often move higher, yet stocks that gap down often move down much more than stocks that gap up.

So far, we've looked at moving averages crossing each other. We've waited 3 consecutive days for the stock to follow that current trend. Then we've looked for it to test the moving average. Here, it broke below the moving average and also had a gap down. There's a better signal of weakness.

Moving over to the right side of the chart, it says never go long or short unless these moving averages cross.

Yet as you can see in Figure 2.1, they started to cross. We could have waited 3 days, and then have entered the trade at that point. But we would have gotten out rather fast because we then saw another crossover.

We've started off simply by looking at moving averages, the 10- and 20-day. We're going to add more indicators as we move forward and create a system similar to my 12-plus system, which will tell us when we should and shouldn't buy.

Some investors detect early signs of breakouts by adding moving averages to volumes.

You'll often find that investors will add a moving average to the volume to alert them when the volume has increased above its daily average (Figure 2.2). This can be an early sign of a positive or a negative breakout. The moving average time frames will vary with each investor's objectives and the market conditions.

Laws of Supply and Demand

You already know that the stock market moves simply based on two things: supply and demand. Together, supply and demand are nothing more than volume. If I have a basket loaded with green and yellow bananas, I have a supply of a product to sell. The demand is determined based on how many green or yellow bananas people want to buy. If green sells quicker than yellow, there will be less supply and more demand for the green bananas. Prices will react accordingly—the price of green bananas in this case will rise to meet the high demand and low supply situation.

When we start getting more supply and demand, we see the market do one of two things. Obviously, when there's more supply of something, we talk about it. On the other hand, if no one wants to buy anything, the stock isn't going to do anything. But if everyone wants to buy something, the stock will go up. Let's take Apple Computers' ipod as an example; so much demand caused the increase of the price. As the interest dropped, so did the price. Another great example of this is real estate value; as interest rates drop, more people can afford to purchase homes, which will then drive the values up. As interest rates increase, the demand for homes drops, and so does the value. It is simply a world of supply and demand—the more we want something, the higher the price. The less of something we want, the lower the price will go.

Supply and demand is none other than volume.

In the chart shown in Figure 2.2, we added a 20-day moving average to the volume. This way we can identify when the volume is moving above its averages. Often, stocks that are trending upwards don't need volume unless they are testing levels of resistance. In fact, stocks that are dropping in value truly don't need volume either; however, many times stocks that are trending sideways need volume to push them up or down. And as I referenced before, I like to see a stock's daily volume increase 1 ½ times more than the stock's average volume over the past 20 days. This is a sign of commitment and will increase the stock's odds of moving, which in return, will increase your odds of success.

So to start, I'll tell you that we're using the same stock that we considered previously. As we look at the vertical line, we see the same time frame we looked at for the short—where we had a gap down and a crossover in moving averages. But look at what begins to happen to the volume after 5 months: all of a sudden, we start to see an increase in volume. Increased volume will help push your stock in the direction it is going; and, the more volume, the bigger the movement will be.

If I'm on to tab 2 of my 12-plus system, I'm now getting another plus, because volume is increasing and the trend is continuing to move down. In summary, we're adding moving averages to our volume; and, as the volume bars begin to increase above the average volume (past 20-day), we're able to see early signs of buying or selling. This will help us determine a sooner and often a better entry or exit point. As the saying goes "timing" is the most important part of being a successful trader. It's always best to get in early and get out early.

Chapter Summary

- A moving average is the average of a stock's closing prices over a defined period.

- The first thing to remember about a moving average is not its precise total—but what that total represents.

- A moving average represents the price of a stock within a certain period.

- There are two types of moving averages: simple and exponential.

- The shorter the moving average, the faster the movement will be—and vice-versa.

- You should confirm a moving average over at least 3 consecutive days before acting on it.

- The 200-day moving average remains the strongest point of support or resistance.

- A bullish position in a changing market means that you should consider shortening your moving average, resulting in a quicker sell-signal.

Self-test questions

1. Which is the strongest moving average?

   a. 20-day
   b. 50-day
   c. 100-day
   d. 200-day

2. Is the 5-day moving average for the following closing prices: 8.5, 10, 10.5, 7 and 9?

   a. 8.5
   b. 9
   c. 9.5
   d. 10

3. Which is the fastest moving average?

   a. 200-day moving average
   b. 100-day exponential moving average
   c. 3-day exponential moving average
   d. 3-day moving average.

4. When using moving averages, when is a buy signal confirmed?

    a. When the faster moving average crosses over the slower one

    b. When the faster moving average crosses below the slower one

    c. Three days after the faster moving average crosses over the slower moving average

    d. Three days after the faster moving averages crosses below the slower moving average

5. What is the law of supply and demand?

    a. Volume

    b. As the supply of the stock's underlying product increases, the demand for the stock increases and the price rises

    c. The lower the supply of a stock, the lower the price goes

    d. Buy signals

6. What are further confirmations of a moving average crossover?

    a. 3 days without reversing

    b. Volume

    c. A changing market

    d. The 200-day EMA

7. If you are in a bullish position, you should consider:

   a. Lengthening the period of your moving average
   b. Switching to an EMA
   c. Shortening the period of your moving average
   d. Stop using moving averages and switch to a leading indicator

For answers, go to www.traderslibrary.com/TLEcorner

Chapter 3

Balance of Power (BOP)

In this chapter, I'm going to talk to you about balance of power, or BOP©. BOP tells us whether the underlying action in the trading of a stock is a characteristic of systematic buying accumulation or distribution. Look at Figure 3.1 for a classic BOP example: it's plotted by looking at the accumulation that occurs above or below its zero line, which I call a level line or center line. It represents this institution's buying and selling of shares totaling 10,000 or more. The more buying you have, the higher the stock will go; and, the more selling you have, the lower the stock can go. And of course, if you have a lack of buying or selling, it's neutral, which often is a sign that the stock will trend sideways until the buying or selling increases.

FIGURE 3.1

ZERO LINE

Zero Line   **Zero Line**

For color charts go to www. traderslibrary.com/TLEcorner

If someone were to buy or sell 100,000 shares of one individual stock, would it make a difference in the price of that stock? Definitely. I'm now going to tie this together with some other technical indicators to see whether it will enhance our opportunity to assume a long or short position.

> *Balance of Power (BOP) indicates whether the underlying action in a stock trade is a characteristic or a systematic buying accumulation or distribution.*

Bullish BOP

Figure 3.2 exhibits positive BOP. As everyone knows, a green light normally represents go, yellow means caution, and red says stop—unless you're in New York, where it might mean speed up!

FIGURE 3.2

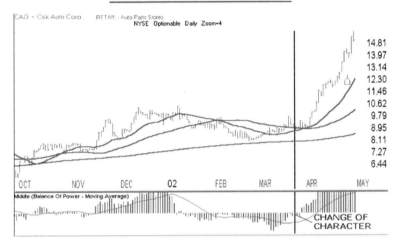

POSITIVE BOP

What we're looking at here is some accelerated institutional selling. I'd call this a change of character—we've gone from bearish, to neutral, and now to bullish. It's a good sign that institutions are starting to buy.

You may prefer to be very cautious and wait until you also see your moving average cross over the cen-

A change of character is when a stock shifts from bearish to bullish or bullish to bearish.

ter line—the zero level. Once a moving average has crossed over and you have entered the trade, there's nothing wrong with being cautious and waiting until it gets to $10, then riding it to $14.

Count on 12-Day Moving Averages

I have found that 12-day simple moving averages often work best because when I've used shorter ones—I've tried 9 and 10 in the past—I've entered trades too early. I've also tried 14 and 15 and found that I've missed out on a low opportunity. I don't mind missing out on these opportunities; there are times in the market where you can actually only get a $1 or $2 out of a stock but I'm more of a position trader and not a day trader. My motto is "get in when it's technically time to and get out when you're told to." Sounds like something my dad said to me as a child, "get in your room and don't come out until I tell you to, or else."

That's why I put a moving average on just about everything because it teaches me to be a bit more cautious when markets are a little uncertain.

Again, you can see a bullish stock here in Figure 3.2. We have a change of character in the institutional BOP. We have the price of the stock above its three selected moving averages, and we have a moving average increasing above the zero level. That's becoming a bullish signal as well.

Figure 3.3 exhibits a chart that shows us bullish volume and BOP. Again, we're using the same stock that we just considered; only, we're adding more indicators to it.

You should start to see a pattern here: the more you use different indicators (provided they are bullish), the greater the odds in your favor. If the indicators are in fact bullish, you should continue to consider this an opportunity to move ahead. Here, we still have the

FIGURE 3.3

BULLISH VOLUME & BOP

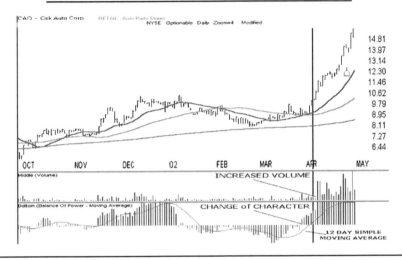

positive BOP and the moving average crossing up, with an increase in volume at the same time.

This was an example of a 12-day simple moving average. If I went with a longer, 15-day average here, I would probably have seen only $1.50 to $2.00 out of the stock. So 12 days is the parameter that I found to work best in this situation.

> *The more you use different indicators, the greater your odds of success will be.*

Count on your Market Snapshots

We've talked about the BOP, which is institutional buying and selling. This concept reminds me of all the family photos my mother has hanging up on the hallway wall of her home. Mom would say that those pictures are priceless for the memories they contained. The same holds true for these "snapshots" of the market, as they'll give you the priceless technical information you'll need to get into and out of trades. This approach is a far cry from the one I relied on when I started trading where, for example, I'd buy Wendy's stock if the hamburger was good.

Bearish BOP

Now, in Figure 3.4, we have a chart showing the opposite—bearish, volume, and BOP—because we know that the stock market doesn't always go up. Starting at the top of the chart, we see that the trend has changed. The stock is moving in a lower direction. There is increased volume, which has risen above the moving average. That's a bearish signal.

We also have a change of character of the opposite side. Before, the BOP represented institutional buying. It now demonstrates institutional selling and, as you can see, it's even greater. Odds are, this stock will continue to move lower at this time.

In summary, we're using moving averages to help us identify when to enter or exit a trade. We are making sure that we see the price of the stock stay above or below those moving averages for 3 con-

FIGURE 3.4

BEARISH VOLUME & BOP

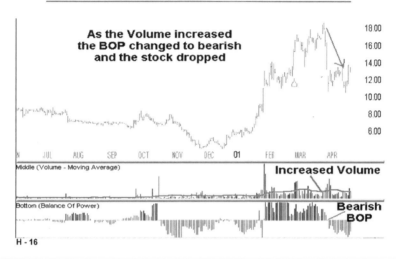

For color charts go to www. traderslibrary.com/TLEcorner

secutive days before acting. We've added some moving averages to volume because we must have increasing volume on these stocks to confirm that an increase is indeed the current trend. And the moving average that we've been using is a 12-day. Upward acceleration would be a positive thing if we were considering shorting the stock.

Using technical indicators provides you with priceless market "snapshots" that can help you get in and out of trades.

BOP Divergence

Now let's talk about BOP divergence—a very, very important concept. As you can see in the graph featured in Figure 3.5, we have a stock that has dramatically increased in price within 3 months, from 40 to about 52. That's a good move upward.

But do you see what's occurring down below at the same time? Institutional selling. As much as we all like to think that we can control the market, our little 100, 200, and or 1,000 shares ultimately don't make a difference. But if an institution is starting to sell, yet its price is moving higher, does this mean that the Stock Market Exchange is trying to trick us into buying it? The answer could be yes.

Simply put, they are raising the asking price on the stock, assuming that people will just accept the increase as a sign of how most

FIGURE 3.5

BOP DIVERGENCE

BVF - Biovail Corp.   DRUGS - Drug Delivery   NYSE Optionable Daily Zoom—4   Modified

PRICE MOVES HIGHER

NOV   DEC   02   FEB   MAR   APR   MAY

Middle (Balance Of Power)   BOP SELLS OFF

H - 17

people buy: "Oh, today it's at 43. Oh, today it's at 45. I should have bought; I didn't buy. Now it's at 45.50; it's going higher. I bought it." The moral is: stay away when you see this picture of divergence with stocks moving up. Buying stocks that are moving higher is great but not if the volume is dropping while the price is increasing.

If an institution is starting to sell, yet its stock price is moving higher (a.k.a. BOP divergence), it's a sign that the Exchange is trying to trick you into buying so be careful and purchase small amounts first to avoid any sudden drop of the stock.

I developed the chart in Figure 3.6 about a year ago, after having a gentleman from Canada, whom I'll call Dr. Mike, come down and spend some time with me in private training. I tested the information in it for 6 months. The observance contained here was essentially Dr. Mike's, and I want to share it with you.

This tight grouping of three moving averages is an indication that the stock price will soon make a major move up or down. That's all we're looking for, right? We don't care if the stock market goes up or down. We may care if it goes sideways, as that movement provides less opportunity. But if it makes a major move up or down,

FIGURE 3.6

BULLISH GROUPING

that gives us a good opportunity to invest to the long side—or an even better opportunity to invest to the down side. The value of other technical indicators will also play a major role in determining the direction of the breakout and a proper entry point.

Note that the three moving averages in Figure 3.7 are all touching. If you ever see this, you better start running to the bank! I built a scan looking for the 20-, 50-, and 200-day moving average to come together and touch, which tells me that this stock is going to make a major move in one direction or the other. There's a lot of opportunity for this $50 stock to make a major move—like going to $100 or even zero.

> *If a scan shows these three moving averages touching at one point, it's a sign that the stock will soon make a major move in one direction or the other.*

As you can see, the key to making money in the stock market is about just finding the right stocks—and the only way to do that is to have the right technical indicators with the right parameters.

Look again at Figure 3.7. If you see a grouping happen, pay close attention to it. Again, I would not jump in and trade this before the rule says it will make a major move to one direction or the other, that is, up or down. I'll use other technical indicators, and when I get to the final tab number 12 of my system, I'll really decide whether to enter the trade or not.

Chapter Summary

- Balance of Power (BOP) indicates whether the underlying action in a stock trade is a characteristic or systematic buying accumulation or distribution.

- The level or center line in BOP represents a stock's accumulation above or below its zero line.

- When a stock shifts between bearish, neutral, and bullish, that shift shows a change of character.

- You'll have greater odds if you rely on many different indicators and not just one.

- Be careful if BOP shows signs of a divergence, when a stock dramatically increases in price with simultaneous institutional selling.

- BOP is similar to Accumulation/Distribution when using other charting programs.

- View technical indicators as priceless market "snapshots" that can assist you in getting into and out of trades.

- When you see three moving averages touching at a single point, consider it a sign that the stock will make a big shift.

Self-test questions

1. When Larson refers to the term "change of character" he's saying the inductor is changing direction from positive to negative or negative to positive?

   a. True
   b. False

2. BOP indicator helps identify:

   a. Retail investors buying small amounts of stock
   b. Retail investors selling large amounts of stock
   c. Institutional investors shorting then market
   d. Institutional buying or selling of large quantities of stock

3. How many Moving Averages is referenced when referring to the term a "grouping of the moving averages?"

   a. 2 moving averages
   b. 3 moving averages
   c. 4 moving averages
   d. 4 or more

4. The tight grouping of the moving averages is an indication that the stock price will move?

   a. Up
   b. Down
   c. Both
   d. One direction or the other

5. If looking for the moving average break outs you should use what parameters of your moving averages:

   a. 10 - 30 - 100
   b. 20 - 100 - 200
   c. 20 - 50 - 200
   d. 30 - 100 - 200

For answers, go to www.traderslibrary.com/TLEcorner

Chapter 4

Moving Average Convergence/Divergence (MACD)

The two technical indicators that I'm going to cover in the next two chapters—moving average convergence/divergence (MACD) and price rate of change (PRC)—have a 90% success rate. That is, when I can identify the exact crossing of these two indicators, I win 90% of the time.

I've been using MACD and PRC for many years now—and they have not led me wrong yet. I created these indicators after many years of trading in and teaching about the stock market.

I should mention that in your consideration of moving averages, you don't necessarily have to see them cross (though it's even more powerful if they do), but merely come together within a certain range.

At least two of the three should touch, and the third should be within an eighth of an inch of the other two. If they're farther away from each other, the process doesn't work as well. Remember, you don't necessarily have to see moving averages cross, but merely move together and touch.

Look at what's happening in Figure 4.1: the 50 dma, 200 dma, and 20 dma have touched. The 20-day moving average, which is a faster moving average than 50 and 200, indicates that we have a crossover as it breaks through the 50 dma and the 200 dma.

At the time that they touch—right about $48—we don't know the direction they'll take. But I definitely would have considered this to be a bearish signal because we closed lower the next day

Lessons Learned by Friends & Family

I've had many students, friends, and family members who have asked me questions about the market or admitted mistakes they'd made. I remember one such situation involving a woman from my church group. I was doing a presentation for the group on how technical indicators would make a difference in their portfolios, and I showed Intel, which at one point was trading at 86. I had just finished showing a gap-down, bearish signal crossing in moving averages when the woman said, "I bought it at 86." When I asked why, she replied, "Well, because I first bought it at 100 and had it for a long time. Now it's at 86, so I thought I'd buy it at 86." Then she told me that she bought more at 65. And knowing technically how weak the stock was it only continued to drop. She like many people haven't heard of a stop loss before, which I'll cover in Chapter 9.

FIGURE 4.1

BEARISH GROUPING

BVF - Biovail Corp   DRUGS - Drug Delivery

NYSE Optionable Daily Zoom=4

and even had a gap down. In all reality, the 20 broke through the 50 and 200, with the latter being the strongest point of resistance.

MACD in Detail

Let's talk in a bit more depth about MACD, which again, stands for Moving Average Convergence/Divergence. It's very similar to the price-moving averages, except that it uses three exponential moving averages instead of one or two.

As I mentioned earlier, parameters make the biggest difference. You can adjust any one of the parameters to be zero or 100—the key is to insert the right number.

In Figure 4.2, you see the typical MACD, which is in the form of two lines. I inserted several question marks when I first tried to use

> *Look for patterns where the three moving averages come together closely.*

this MACD about 6 years ago. I was confused about where to buy and sell, as I saw the stock crossover go up, but then ultimately go lower.

FIGURE 4.2

MACD PLOTTED as LINES

JCP - J.C. Penney Company Inc   RETAIL - Department Stores
NYSE Optionable Daily Zoom=3 Modified

When do you buy or sell?

H - 22

For color charts go to www. traderslibrary.com/TLEcorner

I now prefer using MACDs in a histogram form like the one shown in Figure 4.3 because I like to look for what I referred to before as a change of character.

Take a look at the B&S (buy and sell) in Figure 4.3. You see a change of character in which the stock comes straight up, so you buy. Later you see change of character from the bullish to the bearish side, so you sell and make a good profit. Still later, you have yet another change of character. What you're ultimately doing is adding more indicators to your tabs so you can decide whether you have more positive or negative indications on this trade.

FIGURE 4.3

Chapter Summary

• MACD with PRC has a 90% success rate.

• A stock's moving averages should at least approach one another, if not cross, before you act on that stock.

• MACDs rely on three exponential moving averages instead of one or two.

• Look for patterns where the three moving averages come together closely.

• Inserting the right number is essential to the process of determining a successful parameter.

Self-test questions

1. Which two indicators have a 90% success rate?

    a. 20- and 200-day moving averages
    b. Simple moving averages and exponential moving averages
    c. MACD and simple moving averages
    d. MACD and PRC

2. When does MACD give a powerful signal?

    a. When the lines converge
    b. When the lines diverge
    c. When the lines rise above the 50% level
    d. When MACD is rising and the stock's price is falling

3. When the fast MACD line crosses below the slowest line you:

    a. Buy!
    b. Sell!
    c. Wait to see which way the price breaks
    d. Wait to receive a margin call

4. Which statement is false about MACD?

    a. It is a leading indicator
    b. It uses three moving averages rather than one or two
    c. You can pick and optimize the parameters
    d. It uses exponential rather than simple moving averages

5. What is the advantage of using MACD as a histogram?

    a. You get more buy and sell signals
    b. You get clearer buy and sell signals
    c. The signals become 95% accurate
    d. Visually, a histogram is more unique and stands out when added to the rest of the indicators

For answers, go to www.traderslibrary.com/TLEcorner

Chapter 5

Price Rate of Change (PRC)

As I mentioned in the previous chapter, along with MACD, price rate of change (PRC) is an indicator that has proven itself successful 90% of the time. It's also a fairly new indicator to me, but I've found it to be extremely powerful, especially if I'm patient enough to do two things:

1. **Apply a 21-day parameter:** This is the secret ingredient in the PRC cake. The oscillator is calculated by simply dividing the current day's closing price by the closing price 21 days ago.

2. **Wait for both the price and PRC indicator to cross:** If they cross above the 50% level, it's a bullish signal. If they cross below 50%, it's bearish.

In Figure 5.1, you have an example of PRC in action according to a 21-day parameter. Again, I've drawn another vertical line. At one point, we have a bullish stock with both its price and PRC indicators above the horizontal 50% level. However, the stock becomes bearish once the PRC starts dropping below 50%.

In PRC, be patient enough to apply a 21-day parameter and wait for both the price and PRC indicators to cross.

If you owned this stock and noticed the shift starting to occur, you would ideally sell ½ of your trade right away and the other ½ by the time the PRC had dropped below the 50% level. In a perfect

FIGURE 5.1

ADVANCE WARNING

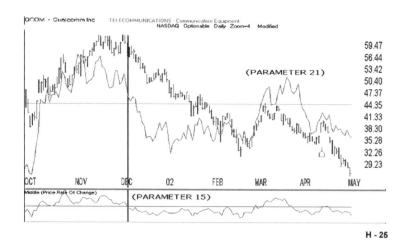

pattern, you would want the price to drop below as well, which would represent an ideal entry point.

The bottom of the chart shows a further increase of your odds with the PRC on a 15-day parameter. Remember, the smaller the number, the faster the movement.

Again, if you follow the vertical line, you see it cross through the 50% level at a certain point. That's a bearish signal. If you go straight up, you see the stock at an all-time high, though with a bearish signal. At the same time, you see the PRC begin to drop. When the PRC eventually crossed, you could have cautiously waited until the price dropped, then taken a short position by shorting the stock or buying put options.

Selling Stock, Let Go of the Past!

I once had a client visit me for two days of private training. As we were going through an evaluation, we discussed what he wanted to accomplish in the stock market. While looking at charts and technical indicators, he showed me an original paper certificate for 1,000 shares of GE stock that his grandparents had given to him. Since then, the stock had kept on splitting and splitting 2:1. When I asked what he planned to do with it, he replied, "Well, I'm just holding it. I want the paper." I told him to go to Kinko's, make a color copy of the original paper, and then do something with that stock, at least learn how to write a covered call against the stock so he could generate a monthly income.

To clarify: if you're using a PRC with a 21-day parameter up top and a 15-day parameter below, and you own a stock where the PRC drops below, you should seriously consider selling 100% of that stock. If you're a conservative person and don't want to sell it all because, for instance, your grandfather's grandfather gave it to you, at least consider selling 50%.

The lesson here is to pay attention to everything—even to those stocks that are sitting in your retirement accounts. I do this with

> *It takes a mere 2 minutes to get a handle on a stock, if you have a system that you trust.*

my wife's portfolio, which is the only retirement account I believe in (where the employer gives the employee a financial match). Once a month, I evaluate the stocks that we have selected within that 401k portfolio by bringing them up and quickly looking at the charts. It takes no more than 2 minutes to completely evaluate a stock; spending just an hour a week to evaluate over 30 stocks has made a big difference in her portfolio.

A recent example of this was Pfizer, a stock that is held by a vast majority of all fund holders because traditionally it hasn't had much risk. But when I recently saw its PRC start to drop in a downward direction, I said to my wife, "Enough—let's get rid of it and find something else."

Pay attention to everything—even the stocks in your 401k or retirement accounts! If you're managing you retirement account that consists of Mutual Funds, you would be better off selecting your favorite technical indicators and using a 5-year chart instead of a 1-year chart. Long-term investments require longer-term time frames because many retirement accounts are limited on the number of times one can move money in and out of certain mutual funds. Plus, many funds have additional costs, which could eat up your future profits. Once you retire and move your retirement account to a self-directed account you may consider investing in ETFs (exchange traded funds), which are similar to mutual funds but don't have all the costs or, more importantly, the management fees. Speaking of management fees, keep this thought in mind: A one thousand dollar mutual fund investment with an average rate of 8% for 65 years will be worth $140,000; yet, when you take the average cost of the management fee of 2 ½ years over the 65 years, the fund value is now down to $30,000. Why is this? Because the stock market goes up, down, and sideways and over the 65 year duration, the management fees eat away at the profits.

Note that in Figure 5.1, we're back to seeing a PRC give us an advance warning. We can confirm it by looking at the two parameters here: 15-day and 21-day.

There are a lot of investors who believe that at times, the best opportunity to make money is by shorting—and it's true that you must be able to make money regardless of the market's direction. So in Figure 5.2, we see shorting of a PRC with the well-known stock WorldCom. The stock starts by trading up close to $15. What happens to the PRC? It starts heading in a downward direction, drops low, retests, and finally says goodbye.

If you wait another 4 trading days, you have a slight gap down and the price dropping below. At $8.86, this becomes a very good short. You short the stock, and it drops down. You may consider getting out when this happens because when you short a stock, you must also know when to cover. It's the reverse of buying: when you buy, you have to know when to sell.

So here, you have a confirmation that the 21-day PRC drops below; and, further down the chart, the 15-day drops below as well. At that point, you short the stock. If you short it at around 14,

FIGURE 5.2

SHORTING with P.R.C.

For color charts go to www. traderslibrary.com/TLEcorner

you're making some very good money and can begin covering when it starts coming up.

When you see both the 15- and the 21-day PRC go above, you

> *When you short a stock, you must also know when to cover.*

may normally consider this to be a positive signal. You see the price begin to move above as well. As I mentioned earlier, you should ideally see the price continue in that direction for 3 consecutive days.

But after 2 up days, this stock gaps down. More importantly, the shorter term PRC goes down. So you shorted this stock again at $7, and now (at the time of writing) it's at $1.46.

Chapter Summary

• PRC and MACD is a successful indicator 90% of the time.

• The keys to the PRCs are to apply a 15 and 21 day setting, and to wait for both the price and PRC indicator to cross.

• Evaluating most stocks takes no longer than 2 minutes—making this important process time very well spent.

• Don't ignore any of your holdings—even those in your retirement accounts.

• When you short a stock, know also when to cover as well.

Self-test questions

1. How do you use PRC?

   a. When PRC reverses direction, that's a buy/short signal
   b. Create a 21-day oscillator for PRC and wait for both the price and PRC to cross
   c. Create a 15- and 21-day oscillator for PRC and wait for the faster line to cross the slower line
   d. Add it to your arsenal of tabbed indicators and use it to confirm previously given signals

2. Why use a 15-day PRC if the secret ingredient is the 21-day oscillator?

   a. Because it gives advance warning for a lagging indicator
   b. When the 15-day PRC lags the 21-day PRC, it signals a false breakout
   c. As a method to test its parameters, giving you the opportunity to fine tune the 21-day PRC
   d. To get a jump on shorting a stock

3. What are the reasons to keep a stock?

   a. Because it's a family heirloom
   b. Because you missed your shorting opportunity and now, according to your indicators, the market has reversed
   c. Because your stock certificate has become a collector's item
   d. Because the stock's price has dropped significantly and now looks like a bargain

4. When using an 15- and 21-day PRC, what do you do when the 15-day PRC crosses into negative territory?

   a. Draw a vertical line to the stock's chart to see if the stock price is going down. If not, buy!
   b. Sell half your position if volume is increasing
   c. Wait for the 21-day PRC and price to cross and confirm a sell signal
   d. Short the stock

5. Mark Larson suggests you review everything in all your stock portfolios

   a. Every day — it only takes two minutes
   b. Once a week, time well spent on the weekend
   c. Once a month, including your retirement accounts
   d. Once a year — solidly chosen investments always go up

For answers, go to www.traderslibrary.com/TLEcorner

Chapter 6

Time-Segmented Volume (TSV)

I'm going to use this chapter to tell you about another indicator that's proprietary to the Worden Brothers TC 2000 program. That indicator is TSV©, which represents time-segmented volume. TSV is a leading indicator because its movement is based on both the stock's price movement and its volume. Ideal entry and exit points are commonly found as the stock moves across the 50% level.

Time-Segmented Volume (TSV) is a leading indicator because its movement is based on both the stock's price movement and its volume.

I mentioned earlier, the indicators I like to use are based on price and volume. In my 12-tab process, TSV falls under tab 11, which is where my strongest technical indicators begin to appear. These indicators are the ones that will confirm whether I'll be trading a stock or not.

In the chart contained within Figure 6.1, we have the TSV along with its zero level (that's the center line going across horizontally). There's a buy signal at the point where it crosses back up. If we then follow the chart straight up, we see that the stock went from 27 to 37. The key is the parameter that we put into the TSV: 18. You may be wondering, can we also use "TSV" to identify a short position? If we look at Figure 6.2 you'll notice that "TSV" gave two shorting opportunities as it crossed down below the 50% level both in the middle of October and then again in the beginning of February.

FIGURE 6.1

H - 28

For color charts go to www. traderslibrary.com/TLEcorner

62 | Mark Larson

Again, you may recall that you can't rely on TSV alone, or any other single indicator for that matter. I typically say that no fewer than 7 of the many technical indicators I'm covering in this book must be present to give me a "go" signal— be it long or short.

A gap down is good news if you're considering taking a short position—or if you're already in one.

Again, Figure 6.2 shows a bearish signal with TSV and an 18-day parameter. You can see an obvious gap down below the 200-day moving average.

FIGURE 6.2

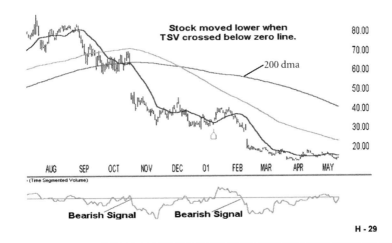

BEARISH SIGNAL

If we come straight down from that point, look at what happens to the TSV. I never would have reentered this trade until a later stage unless I had other indicators that were giving me a positive entry point. The stock then sold off again: if I had considered entering at that point, I wouldn't have seen three consecutive higher closes; so, ultimately I wouldn't have entered.

Later, when we see it start to roll over, that's the TSV saying "get out." You're out again and then another gap down. So we now know that TSV will work for both bullish and bearish signals.

Chapter Summary

- A TSV's movement is based on both a stock's price movement and volume.

- Ideal entry and exit points for a stock under TSV occur across the 50% level.

- No fewer than 7 of the many technical indicators should be present before acting on a stock.

Self-test questions

1. Why is TSV a leading indicator?

   a. It is based on several parameter settings
   b. Because Mark Larson placed it in one of his first tab slots for advance warning
   c. Because it includes volume and price data, and volume tends to precede price in stock movement
   d. Because it uses the shortest periods in its averaging, thus making it the fastest indicator

2. Mark Larson places special importance on TSV because:

   a. He uses it as a confirming indicator
   b. Because it includes volume
   c. On his 12 indicator panel, it is placed 11th as the penultimate confirmation before he places a trade
   d. All of the above

3. Looking at Figure 6.2, which statement is true?

   a. The bearish signal means to sell your stock
   b. The bearish signal means to short your stock. You should have sold any long positions in early October.

c. The moving averages are saying "Buy" and TSV is saying "Sell"

d. The moving averages never give a definitive signal because the stock's price ends up hugging the 200-day moving average rather than crossing through it.

4. In Figure 6.2, how many bearish signals are given?

    a. 1

    b. 3

    c. 5

    d. 7

5. How many indicators need to be in agreement before you get a "go" signal?

    a. 2—one signal and one confirmation

    b. 6—at least half

    c. 7—over half to confirm

    d. All of them—You have to be sure

For answers, go to www.traderslibrary.com/ TLEcorner

Chapter 7

Relative Strength Index and Time-Segmented Volume (RSI TSV)

You are probably already familiar with J. Welles Wilder Jr.'s relative strength index, or RSI©, which compares a stock's gains to its losses over a set time period. You can familiarize yourself with it to an even greater extent by reviewing the chart shown in Figure 7.1

Patience is a Virtue in Market Transactions

After past stock market crashes, I received a lot of calls from clients who said to me, "Mark, I don't know when to buy." I spent a great deal of time helping these people learn the importance of waiting patiently for the RSI line to cross up and over the center line. Their odds of taking on a long position were much greater if they waited for that to occur.

FIGURE 7.1

WILDER'S RSI

When do you buy or sell?

H - 31

For color charts go to www. traderslibrary.com/TLEcorner

Wilder's RSI is a commonly used lagging indicator. When you combine it with time-segmented volume (TSV©) and the right parameters, it becomes a very powerful—not to mention one of my favorite indicators along with the Ease of Movement indicator.

> *Relative Strength Index (RSI) compares a stock's gains to its losses over a set time period.*

This graph in Figure 7.1 is reminiscent of stochastics, which says that one should buy when the stock moves up above the 20% level. But do you sell if you're in the stock when it crosses down through the 80% level? It's a confusing scenario.

FIGURE 7.2

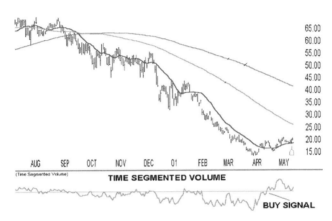

TIME SEGMENTED VOLUME

H - 32

In Figure 7.2 is TSV, which we already know is a leading indicator because it's based on price and volume movement. We can see that there are some positive opportunities to buy when the stock crosses over its 50% level.

In combining these two indicators (Figure 7.3), I've created what I call the RSI TSV indicator. By using three different parameters with RSI TSV, we look for the buy-and-sell signals when we see the indicator line cross through the center line. When this happens, it indicates a good trade 90% of the time.

FIGURE 7.3

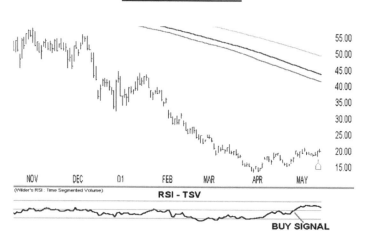

RSI – TSV

(Wilder's RSI : Time Segmented Volume)

RSI - TSV

BUY SIGNAL

H - 33

For color charts go to www. traderslibrary.com/TLEcorner

RSI Alone Does Not Make a Great Indicator

I had a hard time using RSI alone to identify when to buy and sell. No matter what number I inserted, I just couldn't find good entry and exit points. That was part of my impetus for creating the combined RSI TSV indicator, which has proven to be very successful for me. RSI TSV can also help you identify when to exit a trade.

Chapter Summary

- RSI TSV is formed by combining Wilder's relative-strength index and time-sensitive volume.

- Like other top indicators, RSI TSV can help you decide when to get into a trade, and when to get out of it.

- For RSI TSV to be effective, you must wait patiently for it to cross its center line.

- RSI TSV is one of many favorite indicators.

Self-test questions

1. Who originally developed the Relative Strength Index?

   a. Mark Larson
   b. Charles Dow as part of the Dow Theory
   c. J. Welles Wilder
   d. The Worden Brothers

2. RSI compares:

   a. A stock's gains to its losses
   b. A stock's growth to its volume
   c. A stock's gains to the Market's direction
   d. Up days to down days for the past 18 days

3. What weakness is there in RSI?

   a. It frequently gives false signals
   b. It significantly lags all other indicators
   c. It's impossible to find the right parameters
   d. It gives ambiguous buy/sell signals

4. Why is RSI/TSV a big favorite of Mark Larson's?

   a. Because he created it
   b. Because it's 90% accurate
   c. Because you'll never get caught in a bear trap when using it
   d. Because it's the most leading indicator

5. What is the key to using RSI/TSV?

   a. Waiting for it to cross the 20% line
   b. Having the patience to wait for it to cross the 50% line
   c. Waiting for a major market reversal before applying it
   d. Testing it until you find the perfect parameters

6. Looking at Figure 7.3 and using Mark Larson's rules, when would you buy the stock?

   a. When RSI/TSV gives the buy signal
   b. Three days after RSI-TSV gives the buy signal
   c. Three days after the moving averages cross and RSI-TSV gives the buy signal
   d. When 7 of the 12 indicators give a buy signal

For answers, go to www.traderslibrary.com/TLEcorner

Chapter 8
Inertia

Now that you've reached chapter 8 of this book, I'll give you one of my ultimate favorite indicators. The Inertia indicator takes its name from the realm of physics. Used to describe the tendency of a body in motion to stay in motion until acted upon by an outside force, here it is used to measure the momentum of a stock based upon its volatility.

Inertia is measured on a scale from 0 to 100. Negative inertia is seen if the indicator is below 50. If the indicator is above 50, it is said to have positive inertia. Signs of positive inertia are indicative of a long-term upward trend. Signs of negative inertia illustrate long-term downtrends. It's one of few indicators that is simple yet extremely powerful and can be very rewarding if used correctly. One of the most important things to remember about using inertia correctly is to have patience. Always remember that the stock or index price must be trending in the same direction as the inertia when crossing above or below the 50. You'll need to confirm the support or resistance level to help determine the proper timing of the trade. As you see in Figure 8.1, the current setting for the Inertia indicator is 10, 14, and 20. With these settings you should have a better understanding of when the stock is bullish or bearish or, better yet, how to find better entry or exit points. Take a look at the center line, which crosses from the left side of the indicator chart to the

FIGURE 8.1

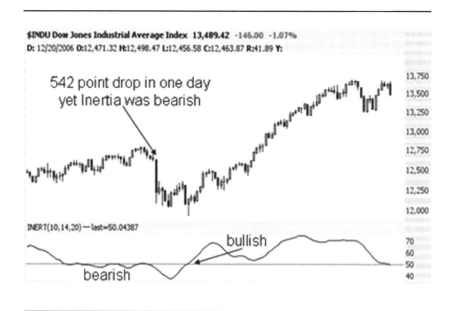

$INDU Dow Jones Industrial Average Index 13,489.42 -146.00 -1.07%
D: 12/20/2006 O:12,471.32 H:12,498.47 L:12,456.58 C:12,463.87 R:41.89 Y:

542 point drop in one day yet Inertia was bearish

INERT(10,14,20) — last=50.04387

bullish

bearish

13,750
13,500
13,250
13,000
12,750
12,500
12,250
12,000

70
60
50
40

right side of the indicator chart. As the inertia moves across the center line, it's giving me a confirmation that the stock is more bullish (moving from below the center line to above it), which gives me more confidence to enter the trade.

At this point, it is up to you to decide what size your purchase will be. For example, if you're a 1,000 share trader, you can purchase the entire amount in several orders of smaller sizes until you have purchased the entire 1,000 shares. As an option trader, I often trade anywhere from 20 contracts to 200 contracts; so, with the size of 20 contracts, I'll purchase all of them at the same time. But, if I'm really bullish, I'm purchasing as many as 200 contracts. In this case, I will purchase in groups of 20 contracts at a time as the stock continues to move higher.

This rule doesn't apply to selling because when I want out, I often place an order to exit to avoid losses if the stock continues lower. By the way as an option trader, I do use the Average True Range indicator to exit the trade. In chapter 9, you'll learn more about the ATR indicator; but for now, remember that the sell order for my option is based on the stock trading at a certain price (double the ATR number). Once the price of the stock reaches this predetermined number, the order to sell the options is executed.

To keep it simple, online brokerage firm **thinkorswim** allows me to enter or exit an option trade based on the stock trading at a certain price. This is very powerful because most option traders sell their option for a loss based on a percentage of the option cost; I believe you should sell your option based on what the stock does or how it reacts at certain support or resistance levels.

Of the many different technical indictors I use, I like to refer to this indicator as a confidence builder. If you look at the chart of the Dow Jones during the year 2007, you'll notice that the indicator was bearish (below 50), which would have helped you avoid the 542 point drop in the Dow Jones. It would have also helped your bullish confidence when the Inertia moved from negative to positive (below 50 to above 50) as the Dow Jones began a nice 1616 point upward movement in a time frame of about 3 months. So at this point, you're asking yourself is this really that powerful? And that answer is? Well, I'll leave that for you to decide but I can tell you this: if it works on the major index like the Dow Jones, wait until you test it yourself and see how well it works with individual stocks.

Chapter Summary

• The inertia indicator is extremely powerful but should not be used without other indicators as well.

• It is said that when the indicator is below 50, the stock is more bearish to neutral and when above 50, it tends to be more bullish.

• This indicator is one if many that can be used on both stocks and indexes such as the Dow Jones and S&P 500.

• Larson refers to this indicator as a confidence builder because it helps him determine a better time to enter or exit his trades.

Self-test questions

1. Inertia indicators movement above or below 50 is based on the stock's

   a. Institutional buying and selling
   b. Underlined volume
   c. Institutional buying and selling and its volume
   d. Measure of volatility

2. What are the current parameters being used for the Inertia indicator?

   a. 8, 12, 20
   b. 10, 12, 30
   c. 10, 14, 20
   d. 12, 14, 30

3. The inertia indicator is helpful in many ways, most importantly by:

   a. Determining a stop loss order
   b. Helping determine the strength or weakness of the stock or index
   c. Better determining when to get into a trade
   d. Identifying the size of the trade one should place

4. When would be the best time to enter a trade once the indicator has crossed above or below 50?

    a. When you get confirmation from other technical indicators

    b. When the volume as increased

    c. Immediately

    d. Three trading days after the crossing

5. When is a negative inertia going to be of best use?

    a. When the stock is moving higher and the indictor starts moving lower

    b. When it begins to point down and move lower

    c. Only when it is below 50 and stays below 50 is it helpful

    d. When the indicator actually crossed from above 50 down below 50 and remains there

For answers, go to www.traderslibrary.com/TLEcorner

Chapter 9
Average True Range (ATR)

Average True Range or ATR is a measurement of volatility. It measures the average of true price ranges over time. The true range is the greatest distance between today's high to today's low, yesterday's close to today's high, or yesterday's close to today's low. The ATR is a moving average of the true ranges. High ATR values often occur at market bottoms following a panic sell-off. Low ATR values are often found during extended sideways movements, like those found at market tops or after consolidation periods. The ATR can be used in a channel breakout method of trading by adding or subtracting from the previous bar's close or the current bar's open.

Now for those of us who do not have the engineer mind, the ATR tells me what the average daily travel distance (up or down) is for a stock or index for a select number of days, which for me is currently based on a 15 day parameter. As an example: if the chart is giving me a number of $1.75 for XYZ stock, then it's telling me that the stock moved an average of $1.75 per day over the past 15 days. So now you're asking, how will this be helpful to us? Well, we're going to use the ATR to help determine our stop loss orders. For those of you that don't know where to place a stop loss or set your stop loss too closely to the current price of the stock, you'll now be able to refine where the actual stop loss should be.

Let me begin by explaining a stop loss order for those who are not familiar with stop losses. A stop loss order is simply a price an investor chooses to sell their invest-

> *A stop loss order is simply a price an investor chooses to sell their investment.*

ment. It is said that one of the most common mistakes investors make is that they don't know when to sell. We're going to help you fine tune that skill and help you avoid the most commonly known term: kicked out.

Many investors don't use a stop loss because once they have chosen a price to sell, it seems that, at times, the price of the stock will drop to your stop loss point, execute the sale of the stock (get kicked out), and then increase in value. This will leave an investor saying, "I wish I didn't place a stop loss" because the stock moved lower, sold, and is higher now.

Trust me—this won't happen every time, and it's ok! I would rather see an investor use a stop loss then not; and, if your stop loss did get executed and you sold the investment but still like the trade, then enter the trade again. The real purpose of a stop loss order is

FIGURE 9.1

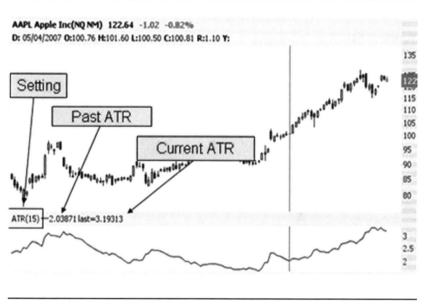

AAPL Apple Inc(NQ NM) 122.64 -1.02 -0.82%
D: 05/04/2007 O:100.76 H:101.60 L:100.50 C:100.81 R:1.10 Y:

For color charts go to www. traderslibrary.com/TLEcorner

to protect your profits and limit your losses. Let me show you an example of a prophet.net chart using an ATR. Then, we'll go a step further with some rules for using the ATR.

Viewing the chart of Apple (Figure 9.1), you'll see I've added 3 notations that tell you the following about the ATR.

Setting:

The current ATR setting is 15 days, which is based on 3 weeks of actual trading. I find that this setting works best because when I used a smaller number, the movement was too quick; and, when I used a larger number, the movement was too slow resulting in the wrong stop loss. As an aside, I have used a shorter number such as 10 when I have greater profits and am looking to exit the trade.

Past ATR:

The past ATR of 2.03 shows me what the average price range was back in May (the vertical line represents that date), which lets me know that the stock's current ATR is much higher. This is common when stocks move higher in price and/or the volatility changes.

Current ATR:

The current ATR of 3.19 shown here represents the most recent average price movement in the past 15 days. As you'll notice, the current ATR has increased over the past ATR by 1.16, which really represents an additional $1.16 per share. Please note that the setting for the ATR is 15 and the chart time frame must be a one year chart; otherwise, you'll be looking at something other than the average price for the past 15 days.

Let's now put this wonderful tool to use. I want to share with you how to implement the ATR for stop loss orders. Once you have identified the average price for the past 15 days, which in this example is $3.19, you know that you'll need a stop loss more than $3.19 to avoid selling the stock drop and seeing the stock move higher by the end of the trading day. My rule of thumb has been to use the current ATR and then double that number. With the Apple example, if the ATR is 3.19, then my stop loss will be based on a price of $6.38. With Apple's current price of $122.00 per share and an ATR of 3.19, my stop loss would be $6.38 lower than the current price. This means that the stop would execute when the stock price reached $115.62 on the bid side. For some, the 6.38 stop loss may be too large, but you must be willing to leave room for the overall market movement while allowing for the stock to move higher in the long term. Also remember, as any good investor would do, adjust the stop loss daily or weekly.

Chapter Summary

- Average True Range shows the average price movement of the stock or index over a certain number of days.

- The longer the parameter setting the less volatile the ATR price will be.

- A very low ATR often indicates a sideways moving stock or market.

- When using the ATR, investors like to identify extreme lows or highs in the market by using the ATR price as a sign. An increased ATR could identify the market bottom and a decreased ATR could indicate a market top.

- When moving your cursor side to side across your chart, you'll be able to see the past ATR prices.

- Using the ATR is very helpful when placing stop loss orders on his investments.

- The Average True Range Indicator is not found on all charting programs available. It is available with my online brokerage firm, **thinkorswim**. Could this be one of the reasons that **thinkorswim** topped *Barron's* 2007 list of software-based brokers for the second year in a row, earning 4 ½ out of a possible five stars? You'll have to decide for yourself.

• To set up the ATR indicator you'll need to right click on any chart and select studies. Apply studies, select Average True Range, and edit your setting to 15 or another number of your choice.

Self-test questions

1. What time frame does Larson use for the ATR?

   a. 13 day parameter
   b. 15 day parameter
   c. 18 day parameter
   d. 21 day parameter

2. When a stock price increases in value, what often happens with the current ATR price?

   a. stays the same
   b. moves lower
   c. moves lower than the past ATR
   d. increases as the price increases

3. If using the ATR for stop loss purposes which one of the following is best?

   a. multiple the current ATR by 3 to determine your stop loss price
   b. use the past ATR number to determine a stop loss price
   c. double the current ATR price to determine your stop loss
   d. use the current ATR price as to determine your stop loss

4. The preferred chart time frame when looking at the ATR indicator is?

   a. 3 month chart
   b. 6 month chart
   c. 9 month chart
   d. 12 month chart

5. When using an ATR for your stop loss orders, should you place the order as

   a. limit order
   b. market order
   c. both
   d. none

For answers, go to www.traderslibrary.com/TLEcorner

Chapter 10

Stock Scans with Six Important Indicators

If you're at all like me, you get tired of constantly looking at hundreds of charts, trying to find a grouping of three moving averages coming together, or an RSI TSV that's crossing up, or a moving average convergence/divergence (MACD) that recently had a change of character.

Several years ago, I set out to remedy this problem by putting together stock scans, which has become my favorite thing to do in the stock market.

Figure 10.1 shows you how stock scans are similar to your mom's prized cake recipe that I referred to in the introduction to this book. In that "recipe," you add a select amount of certain ingredients, which consists of indicators and parameters, to create a perfect guideline for a stock's behavior.

You can create stock scans for all market conditions, giving you the ability to select good, strong investments under those conditions.

> *Stock scans contain a select amount of indicators and parameters that result in a comprehensive view of a stock's behavior.*

As you'll see in this first scan in Figure 10.1, I've used Worden Brothers TC 2000© to build a bullish scan.

I've sorted this scan using Worden Notes. You can see that the stock was trading at 33.52 on February 21. Because this is a bullish scan, the stock should go up. If you analyze the stock, you'd look at the moving average and say, "Okay, it's above three moving aver-

---

FIGURE 10.1

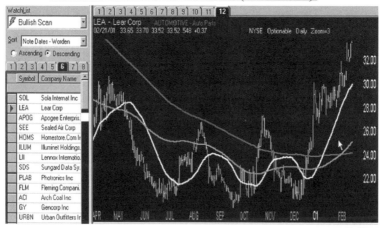

BULLISH SCAN (before)

ages, which is a good sign that the stock is moving up. Oh, look, it also broke above its two recent peaks; it's good that it broke above its strongest point of resistance."

You can observe in Figure 10.2 that the stock we just analyzed ended up at 51.

Because we know that the market goes up and down, we also know that we'll have bearish scans, like the common one you see here in Figure 10.3 for EMC. The stock was 46.50 on February 21.

In this subsequent scan in Figure 10.4, you see where EMC is at the time of the writing—$8.78.

FIGURE 10.2

BULLISH SCAN (after)

LEA - Lear Corp   AUTOMOTIVE - Auto Parts
NYSE Optionable Daily Zoom=4 Modified

51.51
49.17
46.83
44.50
42.17
39.83
37.49
35.16
32.83
30.49
28.15

OCT   NOV   DEC   02   FEB   MAR   APR   MAY

H - 36

FIGURE 10.3

BEARISH SCAN (before)

For color charts go to www.traderslibrary.com/TLEcorner

By scanning the stocks, finding the cream of the crop, and then focusing on the technical indicators in that crop, you have an ideal recipe for identifying which stocks to track. Otherwise, you develop what I call "analysis paralysis" by staring at charts and indicators all day long.

> *Stock scans save you from the time-consuming tedium of analyzing hundreds of charts and indicators each day.*

FIGURE 10.4

BEARISH SCAN (after)

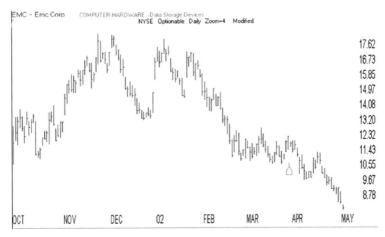

EMC - Emc Corp   COMPUTER HARDWARE - Data Storage Devices
NYSE Optionable Daily Zoom=4   Modified

17.62
16.73
15.85
14.97
14.08
13.20
12.32
11.43
10.55
9.67
8.78

OCT   NOV   DEC   02   FEB   MAR   APR   MAY

H - 39

Patience Is a Virtue in Market Transactions

In the bullish and bearish scans that I covered in this chapter, I had at least six different technical ingredients—certain things that were happening to the stock within certain time frames. You may eventually develop your own ingredients that work better for you, after studying a particular stock long enough and finding the parameters that are making a difference.

Chapter Summary

- Stock scans eliminate the tedium of analyzing hundreds upon hundreds of individual stocks by helping you choose strong investments under predetermined market conditions.

- Though Larson has seen signs of success in his combinations of technical indicators, you may eventually create your own combinations that are successful for you.

Self-test questions

1. What is the advantage of using a stock screen?

   a. You can amass a huge number of likely stocks for your watch list
   b. You can automate your search procedure and reduce the amount of time you spend looking for individual stocks
   c. You can eliminate your indicators by scanning for ideal stocks
   d. You can pinpoint stocks at their tops and bottoms

2. What is the disadvantage to using stock screens?

   a. You develop "analysis paralysis" from using them
   b. You need to tailor them to specific market conditions
   c. You don't find out if they work until you've made a few trades
   d. They only work in bull markets for buying opportunities

3. How many parameters does Mark Larsen suggest you use when setting up a stock screen?

   a. 1 per screen
   b. 2-3
   c. 4-5
   d. 6 or more

4. Why can't you rely on stock scans alone to trade stocks?

   a. A strictly mechanical approach needs the human touch
   b. Computer datafeeds of the prices used in stock charts can be incorrect
   c. The don't tell you when to enter and exit a trade
   d. Stock charts are incomplete until indicators are added

5. What is the goal of progressing to stock screening?

   a. Higher profits
   b. Leaving behind the drudgery of using indicators
   c. Further mastery of the market so that you can think on your own and create your own systems
   d. To increase your odds of only entering into a winning trade

For answers, go to www.traderslibrary.com/TLEcorner

Chapter 11

Three Investment Strategies that Work in Any Market

We've come a long way together—we've learned a great deal about what makes for a successful indicator and when to apply indicators to achieve optimal market performance in your portfolio.

Now that you've used these techniques to identify a good opportunity to either go long or short, you're faced with the task of choosing an investment strategy to go with your opportunity.

I've found that there are three very obvious investment strategies that work in any market.

Those all-important strategic areas are:

- Buy a stock when that stock is going up.

- Short a stock when that stock is going down.

- If you're trading an option, either buy the call or buy the put.

It's as simple as that. The only time any trader starts to consider more complex strategies is when he or she doesn't have faith in technical indicators. And the only way to believe in technical indicators is to look at their snapshots, like we've done since the start of this book.

Practice Makes Perfect with Technical Indicators

If you're new to technical indicators, a good way to practice with them is to find a charting service that will allow you to push one key to access all of your information about a particular stock. In TC 2000©, for instance, that key is N. After pressing that key, a single screen pops up, within which you can type and save all the information you want about that stock. You can even check the option prices, type in those prices, and clip a chart to it. Then sometime in the future—30 days, 6 months, 1 year—you can go back and see, for example, that you had tested a specific indicator in 15 charts, and you were right all 15 times. You ultimately stockpile years and years of important data. If using prophet.net, you can either type your notes directly on the chart or select to have an icon on the chart that will show you your text notes when you mouse over the icon.

Chapter Summary

- Relying on the three simple investment strategies, which are driven by technical indicators, enables you to avoid engaging in misleading, complex analyses.

- Experiment with technical indicators by identifying and implementing a charting service that lets you input salient information about a stock on one screen.

Self-test questions

1. According to Mark Larson, how do you know when a stock is going to go up?

    a. The stock's chart shows an upward trend
    b. When a stock is undervalued and a bargain, it's going to go up
    c. Multiple indicators are giving buy signals
    d. There is a sudden divergence in volume and the stock's price

2. Were there any differences in the signals used for shorting versus going long?

    a. No, shorting signals are all the opposite of buy signals
    b. Yes, a gap down is more significant than a gap up
    c. Yes, you can still go long in a bear market, but never short a bull market
    d. No, my indicators and stock screens work equally well both ways

3. What is the advantage of using technical indicators?

    a. They only take two minutes a day to use
    b. They take the complexity out of stock trading
    c. They are tremendously complex and only 10% of the traders using them are applying them correctly, and I am one of them
    d. They are based on statistics and can't be wrong

4. If I am trading options and my indicators show a stock is going up, I would:

    a. sell a put
    b. buy a put
    c. buy a call
    d. sell a call

5. What is the advantage to subscribing to a charting service?

    a. Access to historical stock data
    b. The ability to practice with indicators until you are proficient
    c. The ability to set up stock screens
    d. Being able to save information and your research

For answers, go to www.traderslibrary.com/TLEcorner

Conclusion

As we've seen throughout this text, success in the market is based on technical indicators. The key to using technical indicators is finding the ones that work with your trading style. If you're a short-term trader, use certain time frames and parameters. If you're a mid- to long-term investor, rely on different time frames and parameters.

Remember, the shorter the number, the faster the reaction. The longer the number, the slower the reaction. If you enter a trade and you don't want to exit on a whipsaw, enter a longer parameter. If you enter a trade very cautiously and then want to have a stop loss or exit immediately to limit your losses, use shorter time frames.

Change the parameters when the markets change from bullish to bearish. Use good stock scans with your most rewarding technical indicators. Back-test your beliefs to increase your confidence.

And, above all—practice patience!

Additional Reading

Incometrader.com is a newsletter service for licensed and non-licensed investors who have been trading and displaying trades. It's published three times a week, so visit Incometrader.com for a free trial.

Larson offers additional educational information at www.whymoney.com.

traderslibrary.com's

Trader Education Corner

TRADER'S EDUCATION CENTER
IS NOW AVAILABLE! GO TO:

www.traderslibrary.com/TLEcorner

AND CLICK ON THE EDUCATION CENTER TAB.

Trading Resource Guide

RECOMMENDED READING

THE COMPLETE GUIDE TO TECHNICAL INDICATORS
by Mark Larson

Traders have used the power of technical indicators to put significant gains in their account. Now you can easily carve through the hundreds of indicators and get right to the ones that make money most often and help you achieve success in trading. In this comprehensive guide to cracking the code of technical indicators, best-selling author and acclaimed presenter, Mark Larson, shows you how to find the indicators that best fit your trading style and reveals which indicators work in which markets. With this experience, you will have the power to increase your winning percentage, no matter what the market does.

With over 6 hours of material and a complete online manual, you will be armed to take profits from the market with:

- A clear understanding of the different types of indicators to know which one to use and when to apply it
- The critical elements of indicators—support and resistance, moving averages, volume—so you will master why they work and choose the right one for the right trade,
- In-depth strategies for using Bollinger Bands, when the Bands are showing you good trades and when they are telling you to stay away,
- How to use the rate of change to pinpoint when to enter and when to exit for the biggest upside,
- How to use MACD in wide swinging markets where it is most effec tive at revealing big moves before they happen,

-When Stochastics are better then any other tool and how to use it to capitalize on potential profits,
-Which indicator can confirm a trend and reduce or remove guess work from your trading plan,
-How to tell when a trend is about to reverse so you can tighten your stops or get out with your profits.

Larson hands over his trading expertise with detailed examples of how these indicators work AND real world examples that show the patterns unfold. If you are using technical indicators now, this will reveal new ways to sharpen the accuracy of your trades. If you are eager to learn about these powerful tools, you will have all you need to get started with an enlightening course that takes you all the way to realizing the gains that are waiting for you.

Item #BCMLx5197572- $795.00

TRADE STOCKS ONLINE
by Mark Larson

Here's a Basic training manual for the Online Army! From getting started to lucrative stock split and option strategies, this guide covers it all. With an emphasis on fundamentals and discipline, you'll find clear, non-technical explanations of how to use analyst's research, rating systems, charting, using options in stock trading and more winning strategies.

Item #BCMLx11154 - $29.95

THE ENCYCLOPEDIA OF TECHNICAL MARKET INDICATORS, SECOND EDITION
by Colby Robert

This encyclopaedia provides an alphabetical and up-to-date listing of hundreds of important market indicators. It defines what each indicator is and explains the philosophy behind the indicator.

Item #BCMLx64683 - $75.00

THE TRADER'S GUIDE TO KEY ECONOMIC INDICATORS
by Richard A. Yamarone

The volatile stock market is turning serious investors into macroeconomic-data junkies. Yet understanding just what the economic statistics mean, their place in the actual machinations of the economy and financial markets, and how to decipher the market's likely reactions to the latest pronouncements is a daunting challenge. Interpreting and applying effectively the complex cocktail of statistical data to investment decision making can be overwhelming. This book hones in on the most important economic statistics observed on Wall Street today and points out the role that each plays in moving markets. It highlights the key interrelationships that each statistic possesses in and among the other economic indicators, and outlines their practical significance to investors. An extremely readable desk reference written from the combined perspective of a former trader, academic, and current Wall Street economist, The Trader's Guide to Key Economic Indicators will lead you through the mists of information, revealing what these important measures are and what they really mean.

Item #BCMLx1717474 - $39.95

BREAKTHROUGHS IN TECHNICAL ANALYSIS: NEW THINKING FROM THE WORLD'S TOP MINDS
by David Keller

Building on the success of New Thinking in Technical Analysis (Bloomberg Press, 2000), this book gathers contributions from an international Who's Who of the field. David Keller, Bloomberg L.P.'s own expert on technical analysis, brings together market masters from the United States, Japan, South Africa, England, and other countries. This new book spotlights real breakthroughs and will be sought out by all investors who use technical analysis.

Item #BCMLx4989159 - $60.00

TIMING MODELS AND PROVEN INDICATORS FOR TODAY'S MARKETS

by Nelson Freeburg

Nelson Freeburg has tested, evaluated and written about the most powerful, consistently successful trading systems for years in his famed Formula Research newsletter. Now - he shares these valuable insights with you in an in-depth 2 hr video workshop. He exposes all buy/sell signals and proven price patterns, then details classic systems that work in all timeframes, like the Zweig 4% and Wilder Volatilty System. Plus, tips for testing your timing strategies before risking real money. With its comprehensive online companion manual, you'll see why trading luminaries like Linda Raschke and Paul Tudor Jones regularly follow Freeburg's guidance - and now you can, too.

Item #BCMLx3377587 - $64.95

To get the current lowest price on any item listed

Go to www.traderslibrary.com

Free 2 Week Trial Offer for U.S. Residents From Investor's Business Daily:

I NVESTOR'S BUSINESS DAILY will provide you with the facts, figures, and objective news analysis you need to succeed.

Investor's Business Daily is formatted for a quick and concise read to help you make informed and profitable decisions.

To take advantage of this free 2 week trial offer, e-mail us at customerservice@fpbooks.com or visit our website at www.fpbooks.com where you find other free offers as well.

You can also reach us by calling 1-800-272-2855 or fax us at 410-964-0027.

This book, along with other books, is available at discounts that make it realistic to provide it as a gift to your customers, clients, and staff. For more information on these long lasting, cost effective premiums, please call us at (800) 272-2855 or you may email us at sales@traderslibrary.com.